Contributors

Belinda Betker
Doug Lawrence
L. Ron Hubbard
Mark Everglade
Bjorn Leesson
Tong Ge
Three Kobold in a Trench Coat
Tomeko Brown & Christopher Smallwood
Angie Lofthouse
Patricia Bossano
Robin Emtage
Jenna Greene
Aimee and Mickey Mickelson
Tricia Copeland
Mehdi Esfandiari
Geoffrey R. Jonas
Dennis Barger
Dr. Leah Brancheck
Barry Kellman
Jarmila Turnovsky

Review Tales
A Book Magazine For Indie Authors

COPYRIGHT © 2025
Review Tales Magazine - A Book Magazine for Indie Authors

Founder & Editor in Chief: S. Jeyran Main
Publisher: Review Tales Publishing & Editing Services
Print & Distribution: Ingram Spark
Designs: Pexels
ISBN 978-1-988680-77-4 (Paperback)
ISBN 978-1-988680-76-7 (Digital)
www.jeyranmain.com
For all inquiries, please contact us directly.

Photo Credits from Pexels:
lucasmendesph-6966604
n-voitkevich-5426075
turgut-ka-471583070-30563314

Editor's Note

Welcome to the 16th edition of Book Article Magazine—our Fall issue, arriving just as the season itself begins to shift the light, the pace, and the spirit around us. Autumn is a time of gathering —of thoughts, of harvests, of words. The turning leaves remind us that change can be beautiful, and that every chapter, whether in life or on the page, has its time.

This edition is a celebration of reflection and creativity. Within these pages, you'll find a compelling range of words of wisdom—from seasoned authors offering guidance to readers and writers alike, to fresh voices with timely reminders of why we write at all. Our author confessions section opens the door to the private side of writing—the doubts, the discipline, the surprises—and in doing so, creates space for deeper connection between writer and reader. And as always, the Editor's Picks highlight submissions that moved us, challenged us, and stayed with us long after the final line.

To the talented authors who graciously contributed their work: thank you. Your generosity in sharing your journeys, struggles, victories, and vulnerabilities enriches not only this publication but the wider writing community we're proud to be part of. Your voices help remind us that the process matters just as much as the product, that the story behind the story deserves to be heard.

If you haven't contributed to the magazine yet, we warmly encourage you to do so. Whether you're an author, editor, or avid reader with something valuable to share, this is your space too. We're always seeking thoughtful submissions that uplift, educate, and spark meaningful dialogue.

Fall is often thought of as an ending, but it is just as much a beginning. For many writers, it's the perfect season to settle in, review our manuscripts and motivations, and let creativity stretch its limbs again. The quieter days and longer nights invite us to revisit drafts, chase down that elusive idea, or even begin something entirely new.

At Book Article Magazine, we aim to honor the full rhythm of the writing life—from that first flicker of inspiration to the long hours spent refining, to the joy of holding a completed work in your hands. We do this together, as a community grounded in passion, perseverance, and purpose.

May this issue inspire you, challenge you, and most of all, remind you that your story—whether published, in progress, or still waiting to be written—matters.

With gratitude and anticipation for all that's ahead,

Jeyran Main

Jeyran Main
Editor-in-Chief
Book Article Magazine

FALL 2025 | ISSUE 16

Contents

A SECOND CAREER BY DENNIS BARGER

Dennis Barger

Planning for retirement from a successful 44-year career in the insurance industry, I was advised to find three to four things I would do to stay busy. One of my listed items was to write a novel. I graduated from the University of Cincinnati with a BA in English Literature and a Business Certificate. Additionally, my maternal grandfather, a high school English teacher, had always given us books at Christmas. This spurred my desire to write a book.

Several ideas were developed, but nothing seemed to resonate until I remembered a story I heard while vacationing as a young boy on the Outer Banks, NC, about German U-boat sailors occupying the cottages during the closed winter months. I embarked on researching this and other similar events within the same time frame. I spent over a year researching historical events, people, and facts to ensure accuracy in the fictional adventure of my main characters. An extensive bibliography is provided to help readers distinguish fact from fiction.

A Secret Soldier's Confession is a fictional story set in the present, drawing on historical events. I created an action-adventure tale to keep the reader entertained. The story features a female protagonist, an international setting, a historical hook, and puzzle-solving escapades. The adventure includes an abundance of location details, allowing the reader to feel immersed in the journey.

After a year of research, I wrote the novel during the second year, fine-tuning it through beta readers and completing the initial manuscript. I received advice from fellow author Dana Alioto, author of Hey Nineteen: A Memoir of Growing Up in Milwaukee, Wisconsin. In addition to beta reading, Dana provided insights into the publishing process, especially the challenges of finding a publisher.

I queried numerous literary agents, who all declined to represent my book. I did not expect the amount of work necessary to find literary agents. This included finding lists of agents, researching each agent's submission requirements, and tailoring a specific query letter to their needs. The process required a comparable level of effort to the book research.

I eventually found W. H. Wax Publishing, LLC, a southwest regional publisher. The publisher designed the book cover, delivered expert editing, and launched worldwide distribution.

Finding the publisher occurred through a fortuitous event. My wife and I were vacationing in Italy, and I met Jason Horn, author of Crossing Paths, on a train. The conversation sparked Jason's introduction to his publisher, W. H. Wax Publishing, LLC.

I intend to start an outline for a second novel. And I continue to work on my retirement list along with keeping focus on faith, family, and friends.

Lean Into Life and See Where it Takes You
Dr. Leah Brancheck

Jogging on a gravel path between grassy fields in the hot sun, my heart pounded, and sweat dripped from my forehead. I had gone on a lone excursion in the beautiful outdoors during a bachelorette party. When I returned to our lodgings, my face was salty and dry. My phone was so drenched it wouldn't charge. I felt amazing. I had enjoyed the warmth of the sun, the brilliance of the shades of green around me, and the smell of the fresh air.

I needed more. With two young children, the only free time I had was in the early hours of the morning. As I ran outside in the months that followed, I saw deer, raccoons, and even a coyote. I felt calm as I witnessed sunrises from the roads in my neighborhood. I came to realize it wasn't just the run or the outdoors—it was the time alone with my thoughts that was so healing to me. My thoughts turned to writing, something I had enjoyed in years past before life became so crowded and full.

As winter approached, I stopped running outside. Instead, I wrote and drew in the morning silence, creating something. My dream of writing and illustrating a children's book began to feel possible. I had no idea what I was doing. I read books on the subject. I learned. I failed. I tried again. I drew many pictures, scrapped them, and redrew them. Finally, I held a copy of my very first picture book, RabRab and the Big Angry Feelings. I had created a piece of art starring my children's stuffed animals to help them learn emotional regulation skills. More than that, I had grown. I had pursued my dream despite my inexperience.

Now, I think back on that first morning run during the bachelorette party. I think about how that single moment led me here. It is incredible to witness how life unfolds. I challenge you—at the risk of sounding cliché—to seize the moment, even if it seems small. Even if you are not a runner, a writer, or an artist, seize the moment and see where it takes you.

Draw. Write. Garden. Run. Walk. Create music. Meditate. Take hold—and go for the ride.

Writing about personal trauma
Geoffrey R. Jonas

Writing about personal trauma can be extraordinarily difficult for some; however, it can also be incredibly cathartic. While working through and writing about traumatic experiences may trigger some individuals, for others—like me—it is a therapeutic way to confront trauma and aid in the healing process. One must be careful, however. Delving into the deep recesses of our memories, into our darkness, can open a doorway to suppressed or repressed experiences. This may aggravate the very trauma we are trying to navigate, making the waters even more treacherous than we anticipated. It is essential to educate ourselves about how trauma can affect us and to build a robust toolbox of strategies to manage the emotional consequences these memories may bring to the surface.

I began my healing journey about ten years before the tragic death of my sister. At the time of her passing, I had been sober for six years and had been studying trauma and Substance Use Disorder (SUD) throughout that period. This gave me many tools to cope with the trauma of her loss. Still, I needed to understand more. My research turned to child abuse and trauma—particularly Narcissistic Personality Disorder (NPD)—which I suspected both of my parents suffered from. I believe they had abused not only my sister, but me, throughout our lives.

I started with essays on topics such as the Authentic Self and NPD, trauma and SUD, and managing grief. It is difficult to come to terms with the realization that you were abused. As I state in my book, children don't know they are being abused because they have no frame of reference to understand it. Discovering that your parents were your monsters can be traumatic in itself. Researching and understanding these topics allowed me to be better prepared to face—and write about—the trauma my sister and I endured. So, prepare yourself before you decide to face your demons, and be sure to have proper therapeutic support and tools in place to manage the emotions that will inevitably arise.

05

Leo Turnovsky's Story – A daughter remembers
Jarmila Turnovsky

"Tatí, tell us the story about the burning plane again!"

We called our father Tatí, the Czech word for Daddy. Born in 1918 in Czechoslovakia, he had a wealth of war stories that we never tired of, especially those from his time flying with the RAF. Our favorite was about navigating a B-24 Liberator over the North Sea when it came under fire from German forces. Despite the damage, he dropped four bombs and safely landed the plane.

In 1938, while studying in Prague, Daddy foresaw the danger Hitler's invasion posed to Jews. Against the odds, he fled legally in 1940, securing a U.S. student visa and earning a degree in chemical engineering from Ohio State University. When his family was evicted from their home and he was unable to help, he enlisted in the RAF's Czechoslovak Squadron 311 to fight back.

By 1945, he returned to a changed and controlled Czechoslovakia. Unwilling to live under Soviet oppression, he and my mother fled again in 1948 through snow-covered forests into Austria, then to England. Tragically, they had to leave behind their first daughter, who never made it out from behind the Iron Curtain.

Disliking England's weather, Daddy moved us to Jamaica in 1957, where he began farming. My mother managed the daily work. Daddy was outspoken, rejecting what he considered "stupid" rules and voicing frustration, often as anger. Living in a colonial society, we were raised without religion and never heard words like "Holocaust" or "Nazi," though he told us his entire family had been murdered. He never bought anything German.

At school, we learned only Jamaican and British colonial history. We knew no Czech or Jewish families, and the sense of heritage was absent. My father openly criticized the colonial elite, which often made me feel embarrassed and excluded. I missed family traditions and gatherings—it was just the four of us.

In my early years, I found my father harsh and difficult, but by the time I graduated in 1971, I began asking more profound questions. Sadly, he died suddenly at 54, before I could fully understand him.

Years later, living in Europe, the question "Where are you from?" drove me to explore my Czech Jewish heritage.

That journey led to the laying of Stolpersteine in Czechia and to my book, Ruptured Lives.

Through it all, I came to see my father not just as a difficult man, but as a survivor, shaped by unimaginable loss, resilient and defiant. Today, he is honored as a hero in his hometown, and I finally understand the legacy he left behind.

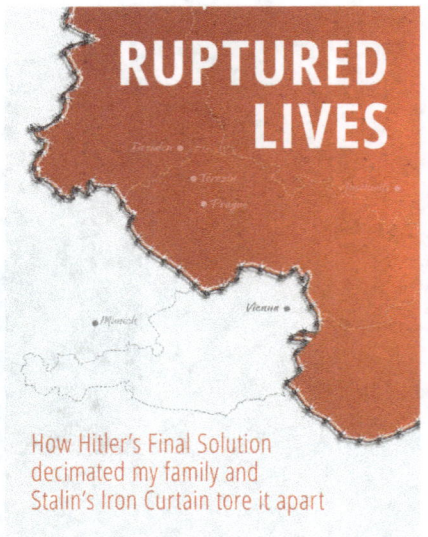

RUPTURED LIVES

How Hitler's Final Solution decimated my family and Stalin's Iron Curtain tore it apart

JARMILA TURNOVSKY

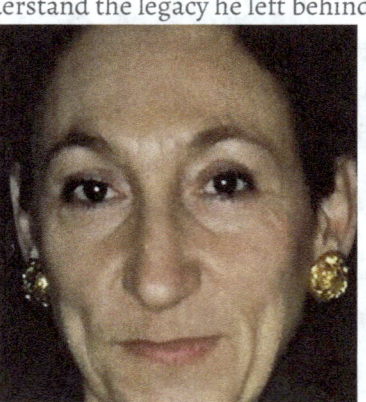

How I Overcame the Following Obstacles to Become an Award-Winning Author

Tong Ge

Born and raised in China, I came to Canada in my late 20s as an international student. While my English was sufficient for academics, it wasn't enough for writing fiction. In 2004, I decided to turn my family story into a novel and began writing in Chinese. However, I soon realized that doing so limited access to resources such as beta readers, editors, and publishers in North America.

Reluctantly, I began rewriting it in English, despite my doubts about my ability. I joined a critique group, took writing courses, and hired a copy editor to polish my chapters. My fellow writers were kind enough to help with grammar and storytelling, and slowly, my confidence grew. Completing a 240,000-word draft, I revised it several times with help from beta readers and editors.

My journey was complicated by a long-term disability from a 2002 work injury, which made extended computer use painful. I had to leave my job and become a commission-based financial advisor, which gave me the flexibility to write, although my income was uncertain. Time and money were constant struggles. After 12-hour workdays, I'd write late at night—my "happy hours"—and listen to audiobooks whenever possible.

Finding a publisher wasn't easy. After agents turned me down, I began querying publishers directly. A mentor from the Borderlines Writers Circle program helped me realize my manuscript was too long. I spent a year restructuring it, and two years later, I found a publisher for my debut novel, The House Filler.

Even with its success—winning the 2024 Independent Press Award and being a finalist for multiple others—marketing remains a challenge. Fortunately, I've now hired a publicist for support.

If I've learned anything, it's this: passion and perseverance matter most. Keep learning, keep writing, and don't give up. I wrote in a second language, with a disability, and no background in creative writing —and if I can do it, so can you.

Merlin – The First Existential Hero

Barry Kellman

You're likely curious whether Merlin was a real figure or a product of a thousand years of storytelling. Did he wield magic, live in Camelot, or advise King Arthur? Fools offer answers; sages don't try. His presence in literature reflects not history, but a need for the archetype of a wise man pursuing peace in chaos.

Whether based on a real person or not, Merlin lives now, part of our cultural DNA. He stands apart from other mythical heroes. Lacking physical strength or overblown magical power, he lives not in Middle Earth or Hogwarts, but in Britain, west of the Severn River, circa 500 A.D.—a time of dread after the Romans departed and Saxons invaded.

He had no followers, no army, no lineage. With no fixed identity, Merlin was condemned to freedom, cast into history with foresight and ingenuity. His freedom was his anguish—acting in a broken world, knowing his powers were inadequate, yet still choosing action. He begins again and again, not out of hope, but choice.

His one "superpower": foreseeing the union of Uther and Ygraine that would produce Arthur. Nine months later, he holds the infant, light yet heavy with destiny.

At night, Merlin ponders how to raise a boy to be not just a king, but the King, gallant, generous. One evening, the Lady of the Lake appears, granting him not spells, but Choice. Most live by custom; Merlin knows he can choose—and that makes him exceptional.

He envies commoners for their predictable lives, but he alone must shape a king. Arthur can build roads and preserve peace—but only if Merlin teaches him discipline and love for the common good.

Unlike other heroes, Merlin chooses freely, not for gods, but for humankind. Sartre echoed this: man is responsible not just for himself, but for all. Merlin's wizardry is wisdom. His seat among mythic figures is not for magic, but for moral awakening. He is the first existential hero.

THE CHRONICLES OF MERLIN

by Barry Kellman

Waiting for the Muse
Jenna Greene

Some authors believe that writer's block is a myth, even though it's been a term bandied about for generations. (I wonder when it was first introduced? There's an interesting thesis topic for anyone who needs one.)

I don't know if I agree with the traditional definition of the term, with the assumption that there is a mysterious, unseen force that hinders writing progress. I think the problem can be simplified.

Maybe the scene isn't ready to be written.

Perhaps the author isn't ready to write it.

It is likely that the narrative is off, and earlier chapters need to be rewritten.

Or the author doesn't have the current headspace to manage it.

Creativity isn't something that can exist under any circumstances. The mind requires a certain degree of freedom to function. When not writing novels, I'm a teacher. This profession has elevated stress levels at certain times of the year. While I can pen many phrases during the summer months, there is little progress during report card season. I assume writers with other professions experience similar setbacks. (Tax season, anyone?) A good writer must be aware of—and acknowledge—the limits on time, schedule, and even mental bandwidth. And it's okay not to make much progress at times. Life exists. Life events, therefore, exist. An eight-year-old's tantrum about wearing a dress in -32°C weather has certainly derailed my efforts at inventing a narrative. And I can't berate myself endlessly for that.

Of course, even when all distractions are removed, writing can still be difficult on its own. Sometimes a scene just won't come together. Characters—feral beasts—don't obey.

What then?

Weep.

Then employ whatever strategy works. I find that going for a walk clears my head. I can think and strategize, and then return to my computer to rework a chapter. Sometimes, the better strategy is just to wait. Be patient. Let the muse sort things out subconsciously. There's a mystery to storytelling, after all—talent wrapped in enigma and luck.

We have to trust our muse will (eventually) figure it out.

The Art of True Gratitude: 5 Steps to Transforming Your Life from Within
Mehdi Esfandiari

How seeing, acknowledging, and cherishing your blessings creates lasting happiness and fulfillment.

When I first began exploring gratitude, I thought it was simply about saying "thank you." However, over time, I realized that gratitude is an intentional practice—one that can transform how we live and how we perceive the world. These five steps have helped me cultivate a lasting sense of appreciation and peace.

Step 1: See What You Have

We often focus on what we lack instead of what we already have. Begin by noticing simple blessings, such as fresh air, a warm drink, or a kind word. These small moments shift your mindset from one of scarcity to one of abundance.

Step 2: Acknowledge Your Blessings

Reflect more deeply on how each blessing affects your life. Ask, "How would I feel if this were gone?" This practice strengthens your awareness and anchors your gratitude.

Step 3: Cherish What You Have

To cherish is to care for something actively. It's choosing to slow down, to protect what matters—your time, your relationships, your health. Gratitude deepens when it becomes an intentional action.

Step 4: Use and Enjoy Your Blessings

Don't save joy for "someday." Use your gifts, nurture your passions, and make the most of what you have now. Engaging with your blessings affirms their value.

Step 5: Share Gratitude

Gratitude multiplies when shared. I want you to please express it sincerely, in everyday moments. A kind word, a heartfelt message, or a simple thank-you can uplift others—and yourself.

Final thought:

Gratitude is more than a feeling—it's a daily choice. When you see, acknowledge, cherish, use, and share your blessings, you create space for joy and fulfillment.

In my book Grateful Lady, I share 444 expressions of gratitude designed to help women build a mindful, healing practice.

Gratitude connects us to what truly matters. Let it begin with one small moment—today.

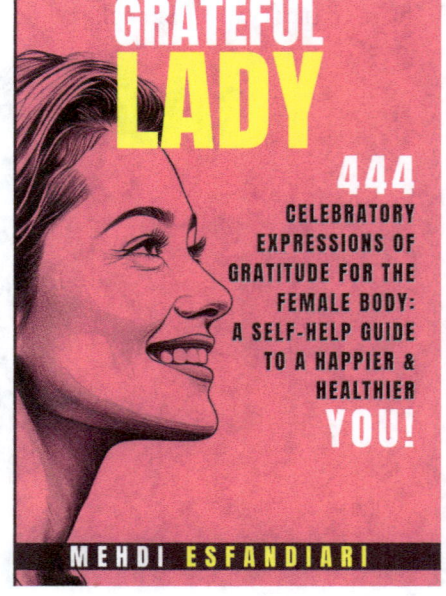

GRATEFUL LADY

444 CELEBRATORY EXPRESSIONS OF GRATITUDE FOR THE FEMALE BODY: A SELF-HELP GUIDE TO A HAPPIER & HEALTHIER YOU!

MEHDI ESFANDIARI

Friends, Friendships, and Found Family
Tricia Copeland

Reflecting on the topic of friendship, two major themes emerged: found family and happiness. As quoted in the 20th season of Grey's Anatomy and confirmed through my AI-powered Google search, the biggest indicator of happiness is the quality of one's social relationships. Friends, friendships, and found family can take very different forms for different people. I believe we can nurture many types of friendships and find family relationships throughout our lives, even simultaneously.

My first experience with found family came during my recovery from an eating disorder. No one in my family of origin had experience with or could relate to the disease or the recovery process. As a result, they couldn't support me during that time in my life. But I met a group of friends and mentors who became my found family. They listened, supported, mentored, and grew alongside me in my recovery journey.

Reflecting on those friendships, I realize that I often incorporate examples of found family into my books. My characters frequently face circumstances unfamiliar to their families of origin—battling unknown foes and navigating uncharted waters. While my first books were women's fiction, I quickly gravitated toward my favorite genre: fantasy. In fantasy, especially young adult fantasy, a key element is that characters need the time, space, and freedom to pursue their quests, often requiring them to form bonds outside of their families of origin.

In the Harry Potter series, Harry finds his found family at Hogwarts. In The Lord of the Rings, Frodo forms the Fellowship, uniting hobbits, elves, dwarves, and men. In The Vampire Diaries TV series, the main characters' parents are long gone, and they rely on each other to face their enemies. In Twilight, Bella finds love with Edward the vampire, but also deep friendship with Jacob the werewolf.

Forming bonds with friends and found family—whether or not we're close to our family of origin—enriches our lives in ways that are hard to measure, even if we're not battling dark forces or embarking on magical quests. So, hug your family and tell your friends you love them... just in case there's a dragon lurking around the corner.

HOW TO GLOW THROUGH EVERY AGE: A NEW MINDSET FOR WOMEN 40+

Robin Emtage

Aging isn't something to resist; it's something to reclaim.

We've been conditioned to view aging as a slow fade. A soft retreat into invisibility. But what if aging isn't a decline at all? What if it's an invitation to glow in a new way?

As women, we've spent decades doing, achieving, caring, adjusting. And somewhere along the way, we're told that after a certain age, our beauty, relevance, or power starts to fade. I say: absolutely not, I refuse to dim.

In my book Keep On Glowing, I talk about redefining beauty, power, and worth on our terms. Glowing through every age means letting go of outdated definitions and embracing a new mindset one that honors who we are now.

Here's what that shift can look like:

- Your beauty isn't behind you—it's evolving. Fine lines don't erase your radiance; they're proof you've lived, laughed, cried, and risen again.
- Self-care isn't indulgence—it's strategy. You glow brighter when you make space for rituals that nourish your skin, hair, body, and spirit.
- Joy is power. The more joy you claim, the more vibrant and magnetic you become. Glow isn't just how you look—it's how you feel, how you live.

This mindset doesn't come from a cream or a number on the scale. It comes from within and it's available to you at any age.

Keep On Glowing is my love letter to women who are ready to rise into their next chapter, not shrink from it. You don't need to be younger; you need to remember who you are. The power within you.

Your glow is not in the past. It's right here, ready to rise and ready to shine.

AN IMMIGRANT'S TALE: ONCE UPON A BLUE MOON, FAITH AND THE SUPERNATURAL STEPPED INTO THE LIGHT

Patricia Bossano

This cathartic novel, based on factual events in my mother's life, begins with her cosmic traits. Knowing where in the zodiac the protagonist (Maggie) sprang from, along with her humble beginnings in a remote part of the world, sets the stage for this heroic romp across continents. But as the story unfolded, Maggie and the rest of the cast seemed to permit themselves to color outside the lines, knowing—before I did—that a celestial something was afoot, and that by the end of this written journey, I would have alchemized our genetic memory.

Love & Homegrown Magic spans seven decades and is a genre-crossing novel with elements of fantasy, spirituality, and the paranormal. Its working title was Daughters of the Bride, but as Maggie's character took shape, and as her daughters stepped into the moonlight, the story itself blossomed into a play on ancestral patterns, traditions, and folk magic. That was how the actual name of the book came into the spotlight.

Thorns and perfumed blossoms coexist in Maggie's magical garden: faith, wonder, heartache, disappointment, laughter, and, above all, love.

As human beings, we all seek ways to navigate our day successfully. Some take a practical approach, while others opt for a spiritual route; others choose a balancing act. In Love & Homegrown Magic, which turns five this year, we gain insight into how one woman incorporates faith, tradition, and supernatural practices into a daily routine of rituals—such as prayer, candle burning, and new moon intentions—to cultivate the winning attitude she needs to succeed. Maggie, protagonist extraordinaire, places the weight of her faith into mundane activity and infuses it with her own brand of magic.

I hope that readers of this novel will be inspired anew to give everyday tasks a magical twist, too. There is magic in a smile, a song, a spontaneous hug, or the preparation of a meal—we just have to believe it.

13

Aimee & Mickey Mickelson

Where are you both from? Is that where you're from originally?

Mickey: I am a lifelong Canadian, having grown up in Alberta. I lived in Edmonton for 23 years, then moved to Calgary, and finally to Lloydminster, which is where I live now.

Aimee: I am a Texan girl, born and raised. I grew up in San Antonio, moved to Houston where my husband attended college, and I currently reside in College Station. If you follow college football, I live in the smallish town that is home to Texas A&M University.

How did each of you get into the field of marketing?

Mickey: I'm based in Alberta and started in marketing after graduating from NAIT. I worked events for Indigo before moving into tech and insurance for credit unions. That's where I met Miranda Oh, the first author I signed. We promoted her book with signings across Alberta and Winnipeg. My autistic daughter helped create the logo for Creative Edge, launched in 2015. Within months, it became a successful author services business.

Aimee: I have a Psychology degree from UTSA, but got into marketing while working at a PR firm during school. After graduating in 2016, I founded Abundantly Social, which evolved from social media marketing into a comprehensive PR and author support service. We help authors hit #1 and celebrate with fun book launches.

What are the roles you both play in helping authors promote their books?

Mickey: I focus on traditional media marketing—booking author interviews on podcasts, newspapers, TV, radio, and magazines. I also secure book reviews and arrange library events and bookstore signings. Honestly, the authors we work with hear from me more than from Aimee. I like to compare it to a car: my efforts are the high-gloss paint and tinted windows, while Aimee is the engine that keeps the car running, handling all the maintenance.

Aimee: Mickey gets you visibility in the traditional arena—podcasts, magazine interviews, etc.—while I focus on using those opportunities digitally to drive online sales and book reviews. I also manage your social media, sharing your latest updates through our networks to maximize your reach.

An Instrument for Florenda by Tomeko Brown & Christopher Smallwood

What would you say is your interesting writing quirk?

One of my writing quirks is writing my ideas on colorful sticky notes. It makes things fun and sometimes gives me a boost in my creativity. Yellow makes me feel bright and energized, blue helps me focus, and purple is my favorite. I stick them on a corkboard and sometimes add smiley face stickers to keep things playful and cheerful. For me, creating a fun and relaxing environment helps me feel more inspired to write.

Where did you get your information or idea for your book?

An Instrument for Florenda was inspired by my own experiences learning to play the clarinet. The story follows a young girl, Florenda, who dreams of joining her school band class. She chooses the clarinet as her instrument. As she learns to play, Florenda's passion and excitement shines throughout the book. The book highlights not only her love for music but also the determination she shows in overcoming challenges. Despite the difficulties, she stays focused on her goal and never gives up. Through Florenda's journey, I hope to inspire young readers to follow their dreams and persevere, even when things get tough.

What do you like to do when you're not writing?

When I'm not writing, I enjoy being outside with my family either at festivals, enjoying the scenery at the lake, beach, or park. I'm all about fun family time and making memories. I also have a passion for crafting, particularly hand-knotting pearl jewelry. It's a relaxing and creative hobby that allows me to unwind and make beautiful, personal pieces. I even had the opportunity to sell a few pieces. Yes, writing is fun but there must be a balance between writing and enjoying other activities that make you happy.

How do you process and deal with negative book reviews?

I see negative book reviews as helpful. They give me a chance to see my book from a different perspective. They might even offer advice I can use in the future. Since starting my writing career, I have learned that you must be open to criticism. I've also come to realize that not every book is for everyone. But if my book can inspire just one child to chase their dreams and push through challenges, then I've accomplished what I set out to do. That's what matters to me.

The Department of Adventuring by Three Kobolds in a Trench Coat

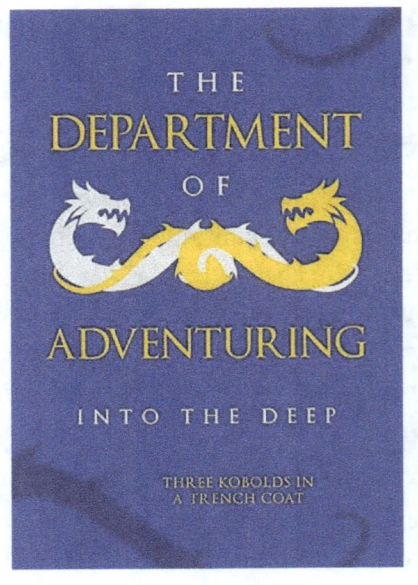

When did you first realize you wanted to be a writer?

I have written a few stories when I was a lot younger for fun but nothing like a book. I did try writing some Dungeons and Dragons campaigns but those are a lot harder than they look, a book is much easier. My first book was the first time I actually finished a story because I knew how I wanted it to end.

How do you schedule your life when you're writing?

I just write whenever I feel like it. I don't force it. The Department of Adventuring was written during my free time when I still worked.

What would you say is your interesting writing quirk?

I try to not take myself too seriously while writing, something I think that a lot of people should do when writing fantasy. Not everything has to be serious all the time. Characters in the story will have out of pocket conversations that have no bearing on the story and even called out a villain for monologuing like in a video game or movie.

Where did you get your information or idea for your book?

I have been playing Dungeons and Dragons for years now. A lot of the elements from Dungeons and Dragons are in the book like spells, classes, and general mechanics. The characters even interact with a few puzzles while going through the final dungeon to the main villain.

What do you like to do when you're not writing?

I mostly watch YouTube videos, play video games on my Switch, and still play Dungeons and Dragons when the stars are right and R'lyeh rises from the bottom of the ocean (In other words, the other players can make it to the game, and the Dungeon master has the time to run the game).

Phases – Poetry by Belinda Betker by Belinda Betker

When did you first realize you wanted to be a writer?

Being a writer, and specifically a poet, was a vague childhood dream, but never a serious aspiration I believed was achievable until I realized in high school that poetry was not just something from the 'old and dead past', but also a modern and wide-ranging genre.

How do you schedule your life when you're writing?

I don't follow a strict schedule at all. I'm a 'go with the flow' writer, and although I don't necessarily sit down every day to write, whether 'old school' with pen and paper, or at my PC, I like to say I write every day because I'm always writing haiku or poems in my head.

What would you say is your interesting writing quirk?

I can write anywhere, anytime, no matter what environment I'm in and no matter what's going on around me. All I need is a pen and paper, and I'm able to write whatever springs to mind.

How did you get your book published?

I was fortunate to have a mentor who recommended a respected publisher to me, and advised and supported me in the process of preparing and submitting my manuscript. Having that submission accepted was one of the most rewarding days of my life.

Where did you get your information or idea for your book?

As my book Phases is a memoir in poetry, the whole book evolved from personal life experiences. I often say the cliché 'my life is an open book', as memoir poetry is by its very nature quite confessional.

Neon Ziggurat by Angie Lofthouse

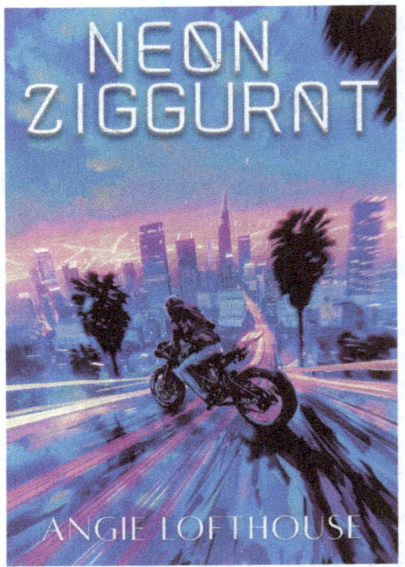

When did you first realize you wanted to be a writer?

I always dreamed of being a writer but never thought I could actually do it. I wrote a few little things in high school, but it wasn't until after I graduated from college that I finally got the courage to start writing for publication.

How do you schedule your life when you're writing?

When my kids were little, I would write at night after everyone went to bed. Now they are all grown up, but nighttime is still my best writing time!

What would you say is your interesting writing quirk?

I write everything by hand in a notebook with a pencil—kind of old-fashioned for someone who writes science fiction.

How did you get your book published?

I published Neon Ziggurat independently with help from a publishing services company, Pink Umbrella, that took care of editing, cover design, formatting, uploading, and everything else. They did a great job and were just the help I needed.

Where did you get your information or idea for your book?

I was indexing some old military records when I came across a bunch of really interesting names: Pressley Pierce, Ransom McCleary, Hazard Snow, Bobby Wild. I was intrigued. The names all became characters in the book.

What do you like to do when you're not writing?

I love watching baseball, hockey, and basketball with my husband, spending time with my family, playing my guitar and ukulele, art journaling, reading, singing with my women's choir, and going for walks around a nearby pond.

As a child, what did you want to do when you grew up?

I wanted to be a particle physicist when I was in school. I love science. I planned to major in physics when I went to college, but the math proved too much for me. I became an English major and sci-fi author instead.

Rune of Whispers by Bjorn Leesson

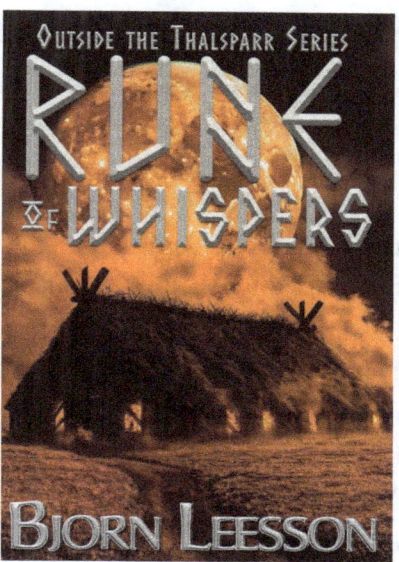

Where are you based? What's your favorite thing about living there?

I have traveled from my roots, but not very far. I was born and raised in the Charleston, South Carolina area until my wife and I decided to move to a location halfway between our real-world jobs—the Sand Hills in the Midlands of South Carolina. I love it here! Low density, quiet, laid-back, and rural. I don't think I could ever move back to an urban or suburban setting now.

With a background in industrial manufacturing, which almost seems like the opposite of creative writing, what got you into writing?

I have always been keen to write; it wasn't until I reached my later years that I decided to really try to publish something. As for the factory background, I have met dozens of the most interesting characters I could ever imagine, and naturally, many of those traits made it into characters in the Outside the Thalsparr series.

What gave you the idea for the series?

A mix of a few of my dozens of personal interests: history (Norse exploration, or Viking Age in this case), the paranormal, and genealogy primarily, with several more to a lesser degree. The story of Myrgjol began churning in my head due to a confluence of two things—my own genealogy and new information in the field of archaeology that confirmed there were indeed powerful women who were Norse warriors and even revered as such in leadership roles. With those sparse beginnings, I planned for a short story explaining this fictitious (but theoretically possible) female Viking warrior named Myrgjol. After two more years and the tossing in of several more of my interests, I am at this minute finalizing the manuscript for the seventh installment in the series, Rune of Building, and the series of seven books totals about 750,000 words!

Can you tell us about the research that went into writing these books?

Inestimable! I drew on my studies of various "-ologies" going all the way back to grade school for this series, so I wouldn't have a clue how to quantify how much research—both direct and indirect—went into Outside the Thalsparr. No matter the actual number of hours, though, it was all worth it to bring Myrgjol, her family and friends, and even her enemies into fantasy existence.

19

Writers of the Future by L. Ron Hubbard

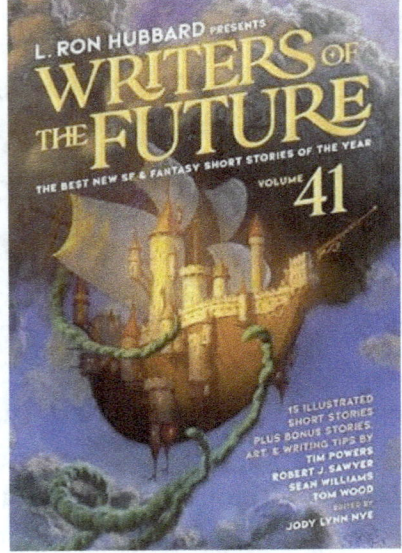

For those of us who aren't familiar with Binbrook, can you tell us about your hometown?

Binbrook is a suburb of Hamilton, Ontario—close to nature but not far from the city. It's quiet and rural, which I prefer over urban living.

Did I hear you were about to study engineering but decided on a degree in English literature instead? Why the about-face?

I wanted a career in engineering, but I didn't enjoy math. Writing kept pulling me in, so I followed my true passion instead.

Have any of the masters of English lit influenced your writing?

Dostoyevsky, especially Crime and Punishment, for its depth. Also Neal Stephenson—I love how he blurs reality and the fantastic.

How often do you sit down to write?

Every day—usually a bit after work and more on weekends. When I'm on vacation, I like to get up early and write for 3–4 hours before lunch, leaving the afternoon and evening for family time. It doesn't always work out, but that's the goal.

When I restarted my serious writing push, I committed to 300 words a day. I still do that for new projects. Once the momentum builds, I naturally write more. While working on the second book in my fantasy series, I wrote over 250,000 words in five months because of how connected I felt to the characters and world.

What's your best advice for achieving success as an author?

Read a lot, write even more, and stay open to feedback. Know your voice, but keep learning.

Could you tell us about a time when it wasn't smooth sailing in your writing life? How did you move past it?

I gave up writing for 10 years. But the characters stayed with me—I couldn't let them go. That pulled me back.

What's your favorite way to pass the time when you're not writing?

When I'm not writing or teaching high school English, I enjoy board games and video games with my wife and kids. We often play Civilization together, and sometimes my son and I team up for Call of Duty zombies.

The lockdowns sparked some new hobbies. We now make homemade pizza every Friday, tend a vegetable garden, and dream of retiring to a small farm. I also go to the gym regularly—I've come to love the discipline and reward of a challenging workout.

Killswitch Overkill by Mark Everglade

When did you first realize you wanted to be a writer?

As a young man, I read Neal Stephenson, William Gibson, and other cyberpunk authors while also diving into Kant, Hegel, Hume, and other philosophers. I knew there was a rich opportunity to blend philosophy and art, which is why one of the best compliments I've received came from author Tanweer Dar, who said my fiction is "philosophical cyberpunk." As a sociologist, I'm able to write about complex social dynamics between factions in a fictional society. I steer away from hard physics, though, lest I misinterpret them. You write what you know, and the more I came to know, the more I wanted to write.

How do you schedule your life when you're writing?

It's easy to get so caught up in the escapism of writing that you neglect other responsibilities. Ultimately, you have to balance work and family by remembering that, no matter how many readers your novel touches, your greatest impact in life is on your family and how you invest in your children. So, you learn to keep family first.

What would you say is your interesting writing quirk?

When I'm depressed, the writing is incredible but so abstract that it's incomprehensible. When I'm content, the writing is clearer but more trite. If I could manufacture just enough depression to be creative—without losing rationality—I might write the perfect book. Music helps me create the mood I need for scenes, which is how I manage the balance.

How did you get your book published?

I was rejected 28 times by traditional publishers, but I remembered that Dune, one of the greatest sci-fi novels, was rejected 29 times—so I tried one more. I queried RockHill Publishing, and they accepted! You must be persistent. Many American literary classics were turned down dozens of times by agents who thought they'd never sell.

Where did you get your information or idea for your book?

My late wife proposed the concept of a tidally locked planet, where one half is always in daylight and the other always in darkness. Light is commodified in the form of giant fireflies used as currency. This sparked my imagination as I explored how the two hemispheres would interact—and used the planet as a metaphor for the human brain: the emotional limbic system vs. the logical side.

Grief by Doug Lawrence

When did you first realize you wanted to be a writer?

My troopmate, with whom I went through RCMP training, wrote a book called Notes from Papa, a collection of motivational messages he wrote to his children every morning. He saw how many blog articles I had written on mentoring and suggested that I do something similar with my blog content. That was the start of my writing journey.

How do you schedule your life when you're writing?

I try to allocate blocks of time for various tasks. These tasks are typically things I know need to be done but that I tend to procrastinate on.

Where did you get your information or idea for your book?

The idea for my book came from being encouraged by others to write on the topic of mental health and to incorporate how mentoring could be part of the support structure. It's essential to understand what mentoring entails and its importance in giving back to society.

What do you like to do when you're not writing?

I'm usually mentoring someone or helping an organization through mentoring. I recently launched a Grief Support program and have been investing a significant amount of time in it when I'm not writing. My writing feeds the Grief Program, and the Grief Program feeds my writing.

As a child, what did you want to do when you grew up?

I grew up on a farm and spent the first 18 years of my life helping my parents. During my last year of high school, I became intrigued by radio announcing. On weekends, I would drive to the nearest radio station to record a segment, which I would then leave for the GM of the station to review. Over time, and after numerous visits by the Royal Canadian Mounted Police to our farm, I thought that police work might be something I would enjoy. I joined the RCMP in 1974 and spent 25 years in the police force.

STAR BROTHER BY MAXINE ROSE SCHUR

Jason is a 16-year-old science genius, yet he's a lonely, emotionally guarded kid. He has no friends, and he wouldn't dare let his classmate Melanie know how much he loves her.

Shunted from one foster home to another, Jason yearns for family. When he learns he has a brother, that's surprising enough, but when his brother reveals a secret so bizarre, so unbelievable, Jason rejects him.

Yet fate throws the brothers together, propelling them on a cross-country road trip, an adventure-filled journey that turns into a perilous race against time to save another family member from imminent death.

With elements of science fiction, thriller, romance, and mystery, Star Brother is, at heart, a moving portrayal of an adolescent yearning to express feelings, find family, and love.

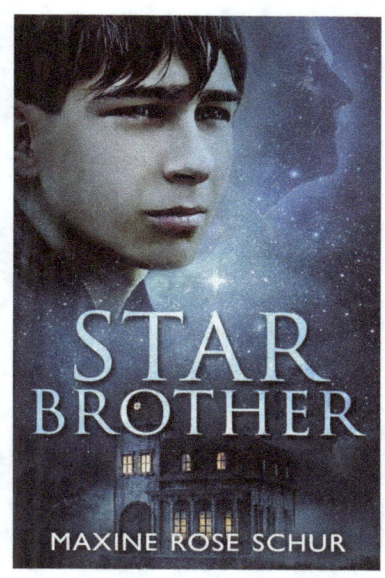

AFTER PEARL BY STEPHEN EOANNOU

1942. War rages in Europe. Pearl Harbor still smolders. And alcoholic private eye Nicholas Bishop wakes up on a hotel room floor with two slugs missing from his .38 revolver. The cops think he's murdered lounge singer Pearl DuGaye, mobsters think he saw something he shouldn't have, and Bishop remembers nothing... Together with his indomitable assistant Gia Alessi, who he may or may not have fired, a WWI vet who often flashes back to 1918, and a one-eyed female dog named Jake, Bishop tries to piece together the events that took place during his disastrous five-day bender. Along the way, he stumbles across a dirty politician, a socialite and her unfaithful husband, and a cabal of American Nazis who are undoubtedly up to no good. Written in the spirit of classic noir, Eoannou adds his own unique voice and flair to the genre in this, the first action-packed outing of the Nicholas Bishop Mysteries...